IN PROFILE

Founders of Religions

Tony D. Triggs

SILVER BURDETT

In Profile

Women of the Air
Founders of Religions
Tyrants of the Twentieth Century
Leaders of the Russian Revolution
Pirates and Privateers
Great Press Barons
Explorers on the Nile
Women Prime Ministers
The Founders of America
The Cinema Greats
The War Poets
The First Men Round the World

First published in 1981 by
Wayland Publishers Ltd
49 Lansdowne Place, Hove
East Sussex BN3 1HF, England

© Copyright 1981 Wayland Publishers Ltd

Adapted and Published in the United States by
Silver Burdett Company, Morristown, N.J.

1982 Printing

ISBN 0-382-06676-6

Library of Congress Catalog Card No. 82-060697

Phototypeset by Direct Image, Hove, Sussex
Printed in the U.K. by Cripplegate Printing Co. Ltd.

Contents

The Buddha

Prince Siddhartha Gautama renounced his crown in favour of the robes of poverty. The young man born into luxury and with the sure promise of power adopted the life of a wandering beggar. He starved himself that his suffering might bring him religious truth. Finally accepting the middle path between luxury and torment, he earned the title Buddha— the Enlightened One— and laid the foundations of a great religion.

Siddhartha Gautama grew up in India, near the modern border with Nepal. In those days India was not as it is now, for the region consisted of many small kingdoms. However, the distant view of the Himalayan Mountains from the rich and fertile valleys Gautama grew up in can hardly have changed, even in two and a half thousand years.

Gautama was born some 560 years before Christ, but, unlike the founder of the Christian religion, Gautama was rich. He was heir to the throne of the people known as the Sakyas, and was brought up amid all the luxuries of palace life.

From the age of eight, Gautama was taught at the palace by Hindu priests and by other brilliant scholars. He learned at that time that all life comes from the God Brahma. According to Hinduism, an individual may go through the cycle of birth, life and death many times. Each new life will reflect his goodness or badness in the life before. If he was bad, he may take the form of an insect. If he was good, he may take the form of a prince or a king. In the end, he will earn his escape from the miseries of life on earth, and enter a state of perpetual bliss.

As well as learning these things from the priests and from those around him, Gautama learned the arts of war. This was expected of him, since as king he

Gautama was born into a life of luxury. His father feared that he might be led away from his duties as future king by the men of religion.

would probably have to lead his people into battle against their neighbours. Killing was not to Gautama's liking, but the arts of war could be practised and enjoyed as harmless, manly sports just as men enjoyed archery and riding. Hunting was also regarded as a good preparation for manhood and war, but Gautama disliked all killing, even the killing of animals.

It is easy to see how Hinduism encouraged respect for all forms of life. It is also easy to understand why the king was beginning to worry. Gautama was his son. He was also a prince and future king—but the teachings of the men of religion might lead him away from the career he was destined to follow. The official priests did not pose such a threat. Much more dangerous, so the king believed, were the teaching and example of the begging friars who wandered the land. He decided he must keep Gautama away from their influence.

Gautama practised the arts of war as if they were merely sports.

Gautama's gentle and holy ways made some people rather hostile towards him. This became clear when, at the age of sixteen, Gautama and a girl called Yasodhara wanted to marry each other. Her father felt that Gautama was not as manly as the other young men. This opinion was put to the test in a sporting event to which all the Sakyan youths were invited. Gautama triumphed in a wide range of activities, including archery and wrestling. At last, he had earned his bride.

Gautama's father was still concerned that, when the time came, Gautama might let his people down by refusing to become their king. He had proved his manliness and gained a wife, but, even so, he might be tempted away from home by the wandering friars.

In those days there were two opinions as to why humans suffer so much, and eventually die. The friars believed that to find peace of mind you must go without pleasures and even the necessities of life, spending your time on earth begging and in prayer.

Others thought you should enjoy life as much as possible while it lasted. The king preferred the second idea. At any rate, he saw no harm in providing a life of wine, women and song for his son, if only this would keep him at home.

Life outside the palace

According to Buddhist scriptures, the king had three new palaces built for Gautama—one for the summer, one for the rainy autumn season, and one for the winter. Each palace was set in magnificent grounds. Inside, Gautama was tempted with every possible luxury and entertainment. There were dancing girls with beautiful bodies to keep Gautama's mind from the world outside the palace gates, a world where cripples died in city streets. The king feared that, if Gautama saw such things, he would turn to the men of religion for answers—and become a man of religion himself.

According to one of the Buddhist scriptures, the king's fears were not unfounded. One day Gautama rode into town in his chariot. Then he saw what life

Even the king's son had to earn the hand of his bride,
Yasodhara, in a sporting contest.

Each of the three palaces built for Gautama was set in magnificent grounds.

was like outside the palace gates—a man old and helpless; a man afflicted by a terrible illness; a body being carried to a bonfire to be destroyed.

These sights shocked Gautama. They made him realize that life is full of grief and torment. His own life of pleasure was not a normal one and would be brought to an end like any other by illness and death. This could happen at any time.

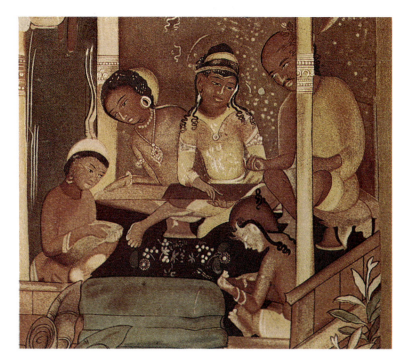

Since childhood, Gautama had been taught that contentment came through hardship and prayer.

When he went into town on another occasion, he met a wandering preacher who, he noticed, was calm and composed. This impressed him greatly. These friars had to live by begging. Even so, they did not seem resentful, or restless, or full of suffering. Instead, they seemed to understand the harshness of life in a way that gave them peace. Life was brief; even so, the friars seemed to live it slowly. Gautama began to think these preachers were right when they taught that peace and understanding come through hardship and prayer. He realized that people who try to enjoy themselves do not find contentment.

Gautama decided that he, too, would live as a holy man, though it meant forsaking his wife and their new-born son, Rahula. He would forsake three magnificent banqueting halls for a simple wooden begging bowl. He was twenty-nine when he made this decision. Breaking the news to Yasodhara could not have been easy, but Gautama must have found it harder still to tell his father.

11

'Middle way' brings enlightenment

Gautama leaves home and becomes a begging holy man . . . He seeks the truth about life and death . . . Joining with other hermits, he fasts till he almost kills himself . . . He adopts the 'middle way' . . . Meditation brings him visions and Enlightenment . . . He still believes in constant rebirth, but now he has a way of escape.

The night Gautama left home his dancing-girls performed as usual, but Gautama was now so ready to give up pleasures like this that he fell asleep before they had finished. He happened to wake while the lamps of scented oil were still flickering. The girls were now asleep all over the floor. To Gautama they were a sprawling, snoring mass of ugliness. Their beauty was no more than jewels and fancy clothes. When he realized this, he was more determined than ever to leave a world where people lusted after trash. He would end his life of luxury and wealth by galloping off that very night.

Gautama could not resist going to Yasodhara's room to look at Rahula. He vowed to return and see him again, but not till prayer and poverty had brought him the wisdom he was searching for.

He rode away with a servant called Channa. At last, after many hours riding through the moonlit night, they reached a river called Anoma, and waded across it. Gautama stopped on the opposite shore and asked Channa to lend him his sword. Channa watched with tears in his eyes as Gautama used it to cut off his beautiful hair. (The holy men were always close-

The dancing girls asleep on the floor, Gautama took his leave of his home and all its luxuries.

For a week Gautama slept in the forest in hollows at the foot of the trees.

cropped.) Gautama changed his princely clothes for the simple robe of a hermit and wandered into the forest, leaving Channa to take his clothes and jewels back to the city. Channa did so, weeping. He would never see Gautama again.

Gautama spent a week in the forest, sleeping by night in hollows at the foot of the trees. He then walked for several days till he reached the capital of the kingdom of Magadha. There, he begged in the streets. But the scraps that were put in his begging bowl looked so revolting they made him feel sick. Perhaps he had never seen the food that was thrown out of his palace kitchens. As the scraps were the only food he could get, he forced himself to chew and swallow them.

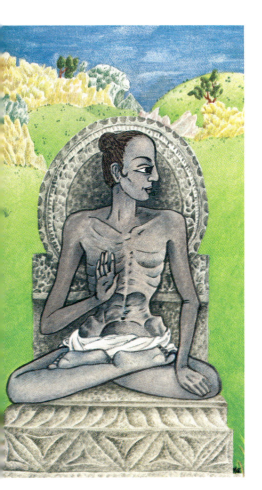

Eating no more than a grain of rice a day, Gautama grew so thin that he could feel his backbone through the front of his stomach.

He met the king and promised him that one day he would return to Madagha and preach to the people. First, though, he must learn from others. He entered monasteries and received instruction from the monks. They admired how quickly he learned, but Gautama was not convinced that their teaching was right. He wondered whether it really showed the people how to escape from the cycle of death and rebirth.

Gautama's path to enlightenment

Gautama left the monasteries and wandered to the village of Uruvela. There, he joined a group of five other hermits who also disliked the pleasure-seeking life of ordinary people. They had gone to the other extreme, and were seeking suffering. One of their ways of achieving this was by starving themselves. They ate far less than they could have got by begging —perhaps as little as a handful of beans in twenty-four hours.

Gautama became so wasted away it is said he could feel his backbone through the front of his stomach. He reduced his daily ration of food to a single seed or grain of rice. As he starved he suffered terrible pain. When he finally collapsed and fell unconscious people thought he was dead. The rumour spread, but Gautama recovered and appeared in the streets with his begging bowl. He had made up his mind to eat as much as he needed to stay in good health. He was no longer willing to suffer, as his companions were and they went on their way without him.

Gautama had discovered 'the middle way' between enjoying a life of luxury and enduring a life of torment. Gautama had now experienced both, and he realized that striving to suffer is just as wrong as yearning for pleasure. Wanting and striving are wrong in themselves. He had realized that before, but

Enlightenment finally came to Gautama after long weeks of meditation beneath a banyan tree.

now he saw that it even applied to suffering.

Gautama's great enlightenment was still to come. Sensing that he was about to acquire this wisdom, he sat beneath a banyan tree and vowed that he would stay there until he had done so. He then began to meditate—to control and use his mind in a way that would bring religious knowledge.

After a long period of meditation (four weeks, according to some accounts), he became aware of the previous lives he had lived. He remembered the names he had had and the different tribes of which he had been a member. He remembered how he had earned his living and how he had met his death. This was part of his enlightenment, for it helped him to understand his own existence.

The Buddha resisted all those temptations which the world takes as its natural pleasures.

He then had a similar vision of the lives of the other men and creatures in the universe. This confirmed his belief that everyone undergoes death and rebirth. It also confirmed that each life reflects the life before.

Finally, Gautama saw clearly that every life, from birth to death, is full of suffering. Pleasures are worthless—a party is just a commotion between the planning and the clearing up! Suffering is caused by desire, which prevents contentment and fuels the process of constant rebirth. Understanding this will help us escape from the cycle of suffering. It will lead us to abandon desires and allow contentment and generosity to take their place.

Gautama had gained enlightenment. He was now the Buddha—the Enlightened One. He would never be born again, for through his visions he had gained understanding and total contentment. His practice in the past had also helped to make him contented. At the end of his life he would enter the timeless heaven-like state he called *nirvana*.

The Buddha gains converts

The Buddha gathers converts to his new religion . . . Organized on a monastic basis, it flourishes during the Buddha's lifetime . . . His death brings the building of monuments—the first pagodas . . . He is credited with special powers . . . In various forms, the religion he founded continues to spread.

The Buddha decided to help other people escape the cycle of death and rebirth. If they understood him properly, and calmed their desires, they too would attain *nirvana.*

He worked out a way of living and thinking for those who would follow his new religion. His first disciples were the five men who had abandoned him when he chose to give up starving himself. He told them they must have the right understanding and thoughts. This meant understanding and sharing the Buddha's ideas. They must also speak, act and live in a kind and considerate way. Finally, they must meditate properly. This would help them to see the truth of the Buddha's ideas. The combination of tranquil lives, correct meditation and right ideas was the way to *nirvana.*

The Buddha kept his promise to preach in Magadha. The king was one of his converts and soon the royal family of his own tribe, the Sakyas, were following suit. The Buddha's father was the first to be converted, in spite of the way he had formerly tried to hinder his son's search for wisdom. Perhaps what impressed him most was the sight of his son coming into the city surrounded by followers. They now numbered thousands. Worldly glory still impressed the king of the Sakyas more than perhaps it should have done.

Devadatta's murder attempts

The Buddha kept his vow to visit Rahula (who was now a young man) and Rahula was converted too. So was the Buddha's cousin, Devadatta, but Devadatta could never control his desire for power—he wanted to take the Buddha's place. He tried to murder his cousin. It is said that he sent a rock crashing down a mountainside towards the Buddha. But the rock broke in two; one half passed to the Buddha's left and one to his right.

Devadatta sent a rock crashing down the mountainside towards the Buddha, but the rock broke in two and the Buddha was saved.

Another story tells of how Devadatta sent a wild elephant charging towards the Buddha in the hope that it would crush him beneath its feet. It ran straight at him down a crowded street. His followers fled, but the Buddha stood and faced it with such repose that the elephant was overcome, and knelt before him.

Stories like this suggest that those who wrote them, after the Buddha's death, had come to regard him as some sort of god. Even during his lifetime the Buddha commanded so much respect that, to follow him, many people left their homes. They were doing what the Buddha had done many years before. Others had already chosen the homeless life of religion. They flocked to the Buddha because they believed he had found the answers they had all been seeking. The Buddha's early followers were men,

The Buddha's early followers were men. He later formed an order of nuns.

Each rainy season, the Buddha accepted the hospitality of a rich man or king.

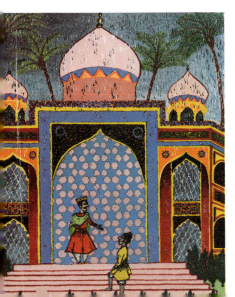

and he formed them into an order of monks. Later, after pressure from various women, including his stepmother, he also formed an order of nuns.

Their lives were partly ruled by the seasons. For most of the year they wandered from place to place, either singly or in little groups. They begged and preached in the open air, and slept in the open air as well, unless they were asked into people's houses. They were rarely refused hospitality.

In July, the scorching summer came to an end. The monsoons began, and travel became impossible. Even during the three months' monsoon, hospitality was freely offered. Some of the Buddha's followers had kept their homes and felt it an honour and blessing to shelter a monk or a nun.

The Buddha spent each rainy season with a rich man or king. Famous people were always pleased to entertain equally famous guests, but the Buddha could only stay with one, even though this caused disappointment and jealousy. The Buddha would have used this as a lesson to his close disciples in the

19

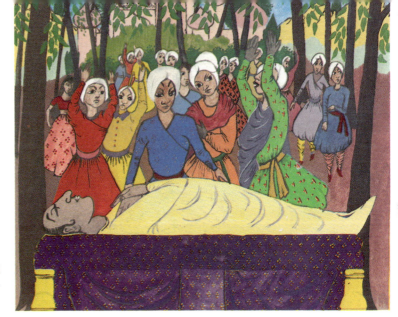

For six days the crowds paid homage to the dead Buddha in the grove of sal trees where his body lay.

The spread of the Buddhist faith brought the building of temples throughout Asia.

harmfulness of human desires.

As time went by, the monks and nuns acquired monastery buildings, given by wealthy supporters and often set in beautiful gardens. Needless to say, the monks and nuns had separate buildings in separate grounds. Love would have led to excessive desires!

The Buddha lived to be eighty. He died of accidental poisoning after eating a meal prepared by a well-meaning blacksmith.

The people of Kusinara, the town where his death occurred, were deeply upset. They came in a crowd to the grove of sal trees where his body lay. For six days they paid him homage, dancing, singing hymns and playing music, then they carried his body through the town and out by the eastern gate. There, with further ritual, they placed his body on the funeral pyre. At last the fire was lit and his flesh was burned away. The bones remained and were divided up and taken to surrounding towns. Stone mounds were built above them, and these became places of pilgrimage as the belief in the Buddha's special saintliness developed.

These mounds gave the Buddhist faith a solidity and reality and reminded people that the Buddha was

Thailand has at least 20,000 Buddhist temple-monastery complexes which form the hub of village life.

special. As the faith spread, monuments were built in other parts of Asia too. These were really the first pagodas.

Nowadays there are several types of Buddhism, most of them based on the early teachings and ways of life. Theravada Buddhism sticks closely to the Buddha's personal teaching and example. This is the old monastic type. It sees the Buddha as a special man, but not a god. Mahayana Buddhism expands his teaching and suits it to the masses who wish to be Buddhists without being monks. This type of Buddhism does see the Buddha as a sort of god.

In the form known as Zen, Mahayana Buddhism is popular in Japan. It is also the favourite type among Buddhist converts in Europe and America. Zen Buddhists emphasize meditation as a way of reaching the 'Buddha-nature' which they say is part of each human being.

Buddhism is the principal religion in Ceylon, Tibet and south-east Asia. It is well established in Japan and China, and seems to be spreading in India, Britain and the USA. In many ways, the modern world, threatened by war and whipped into selfish desires by advertising, seems to envy the ancient Buddhist traditions of peace, kindness and self-denial.

Dates and events

There are no existing records of the Buddha's life written earlier than 236 years after the prophet's death. Historians have been able to establish the pattern of the Buddha's life with reference to accounts written in various languages and the following dates of the major events in Buddha's life are accepted by most authorities.

563 BC   Buddha, then Siddhartha Gautama, is born the son of the king of the Sakya tribe at Kapilavastu, 160 kilometres north of Benares.

533 BC   He leaves his father's court to become a begging holy man.

527 BC   He discovers the 'middle way' and becomes Buddha.

483 BC   Death of Buddha at Kusinagara in Oudh.

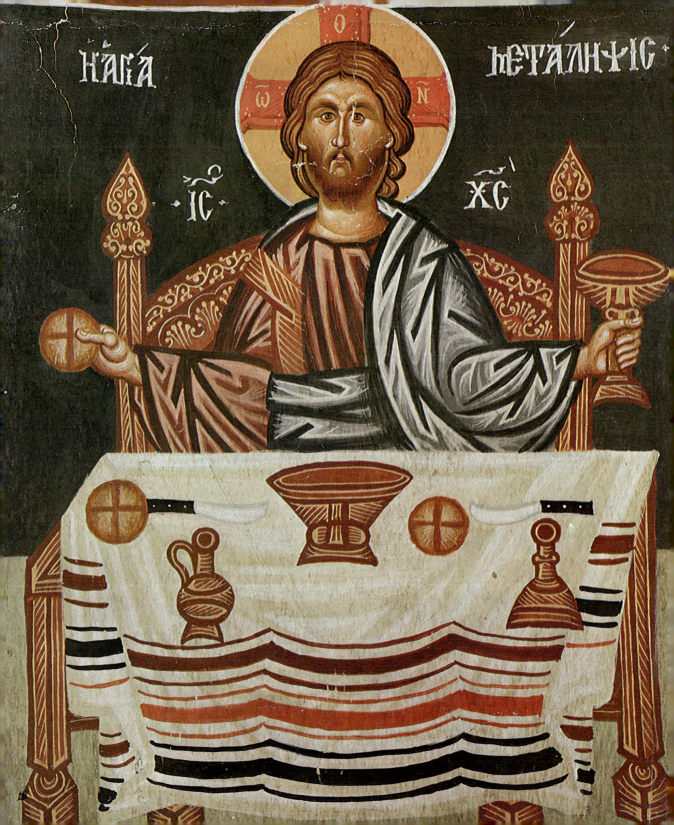

Jesus Christ

The man who lived a life of poverty and suffered the death of a criminal on a Roman gallows is now hailed Son of God, King of Kings and Prince of Peace. Some of Jesus's fellow Jews had wanted him as their King—a man who would lead their nation from the occupation of the Romans—but many more had clamoured for his crucifixion. Even today, after nearly 2000 years, people argue about the life and teachings of this prophet.

Jesus Christ, in his short life gained neither power on earth nor great wealth; he was virtually unknown except for the small section of the world in which he lived and died. And yet few men who have ever lived have had as much influence over as many people as he has. His followers exist today by the millions in every country in the world—the book containing his story is the all time best seller—even time is divided by his birth—and yet all he was in this life was a poor carpenter turned preacher. In order to understand the great impact that this man had, it is important to look at his life and his teachings.

Jesus' birth and childhood

He was born to a woman named Mary and a man named Joseph at some time about 6-4BC. He was born a Hebrew at a time when the Romans were ruling their land. It is interesting to note that there is not a record of where he was born. There would have been little point to note the birth of a poor Jewish boy, son of a carpenter. Tradition tells us however that he was born in Bethlehem. Mary and Joseph were living in Nazareth at that time. Just prior to his birth a census

We cannot be sure whether Jesus was born in Nazareth or Bethlehem.

Jesus listened intelligently to the teachers and priests in the Temple.

was ordered to be taken of all the inhabitants under Roman rule. In order to be counted, people had to return to the town from which their families had originally come. Joseph was of the family of David and so he and Mary travelled to Bethlehem to register. It is believed that Jesus was born there during the census.

There is also little information available to us about his boyhood. Joseph was a carpenter and it is assumed that Jesus learned to be a carpenter from his father as was the custom of the day. In the Gospel of Luke there is a story told of Jesus when he was about 12 years old. We don't know whether this actually happened but, it does reflect something of what Jesus' later life would be.

The journey to Jerusalem

Because Mary and Joseph were Jewish they celebrated the feast of the Passover. For this feast they travelled to Jerusalem to worship at the temple there. On their way home from the feast Mary and Joseph discovered that Jesus was not with them. They quickly returned to Jerusalem where we are told, they searched for him for three days before finding him in the temple. He was listening to the teachers and priests there and discussing with them topics that should have been far beyond the knowledge of a young boy with his background. And yet he was able to do so. The teachers and priests were most impressed with his intelligence and ability to answer their questions.

His parents were confused and asked him why he had stayed behind, and what he was doing at the temple. He answered them that he had to be about his father's work. Christians believe that Joseph was only the foster father of Jesus. They believe that Jesus is the son of God and so it was God's work that

Jesus was beginning to do in the temple. Jesus would spend the last years of his life also doing God's work.

Mary and Joseph had feared something terrible had happened to Jesus. You can imagine the joy that they felt in finding him. This time when they left Jerusalem for Nazareth they made certain that Jesus was with them.

When Jesus was about thirty, he began his work as a preacher and healer.

Jesus returned to Nazareth with his parents where he spent his boyhood and early adulthood growing up and doing all of the normal things a young man would do at that time. He was not seen as extraordinary by any of the people who knew him. As a matter of fact, when Jesus did become well known as a preacher and teacher, and it was thought that he might be the Messiah (Messiah is the name given to a person whom the Jewish people believed would be sent by God to free them from their enemies) the people of Nazareth could not believe it. They had known him for years and never thought there was anything special about him at all.

Jesus and a loving God

Jesus spent his ministry travelling around the countryside preaching to the people. As frequently happens with great leaders, he soon had a group of people who followed him. They listened to what he had to say and they began to believe in a new idea of what God was like.

The people in those days often thought of God as someone who could and would punish them. But Jesus told everyone that God was just like a loving father. He told them how much God loved them, even when they sinned. Jesus said that God's love was like that of a shepherd for his sheep. When a shepherd loses one of his flock, he searches and searches until the lost sheep is found. Jesus told his followers that when the shepherd finds his lost sheep, he is happy, not angry. Jesus said that God loved his people even more than a shepherd loves his flock.

As Jesus travelled and spoke to the people, his message was essentially the same. He reminded people of how much God loved them, and he encouraged people to love each other.

Just as this shepherd rejoiced in finding his lost sheep, so God welcomes back those people who go astray.

Zacchaeus, the tax-collector, climbed a tree to get a better view of Jesus.

Zacchaeus, the Tax Collector

Jesus' love was for all men—for even those who were outcasts hated by the people. One of these was a man called Zacchaeus. Zacchaeus was a tax collector, a position that has always been unpopular with the people. The poor were taxed heavily and often unfairly. Some of what the tax collectors received went into their own pockets and so they were scorned.

One day Jesus was coming to the town where

The Jews discover a peaceful Messiah

Jesus makes friends with rogues and protects poor sinners . . . He is baptized by his cousin John . . . He chooses his twelve disciples . . . He gains fame as a performer of miracles, and as a healer able to raise the dead to life.

Zacchaeus lived. Zacchaeus had heard about Jesus and was anxious to see him. As Jesus and his followers were coming into town, Zacchaeus climbed a tree to get a better look. Jesus saw him and said, 'Come down Zacchaeus—I'm going to eat at your house today.' That was a shock for everyone! Zacchaeus was certainly surprised, but thrilled that someone as famous as Jesus would come and stay with him. Jesus' followers on the other hand were angry. How could Jesus be good to a man like Zacchaeus!

Zacchaeus and Jesus did eat together that day and Zacchaeus was so moved by Jesus' words of compassion and forgiveness that Zacchaeus promised to give back four times what he had cheated from the people. It was quite a change for Zacchaeus.

Jesus, a man of peace

Another time that Jesus surprised his followers concerned a woman who had sinned. The law said she should be stoned to death. Jesus came upon the scene just as the men were about to stone her. Jesus felt sorry for her. He stepped in and said to those who were about to kill her 'Let whichever one of you who has never done anything wrong throw the first stone.' The men were stunned. All of them had done wrong at some time in their lives. We are told that they all turned and left. Jesus told the woman to go her way and sin no more.

While Jesus was becoming well known for his kindness and compassion, he was also becoming famous for his miraculous powers. Wherever he travelled people came to him to be healed—the lame, those who could not hear or speak, those who could not walk, those who were blind, lepers—all of these Jesus cured.

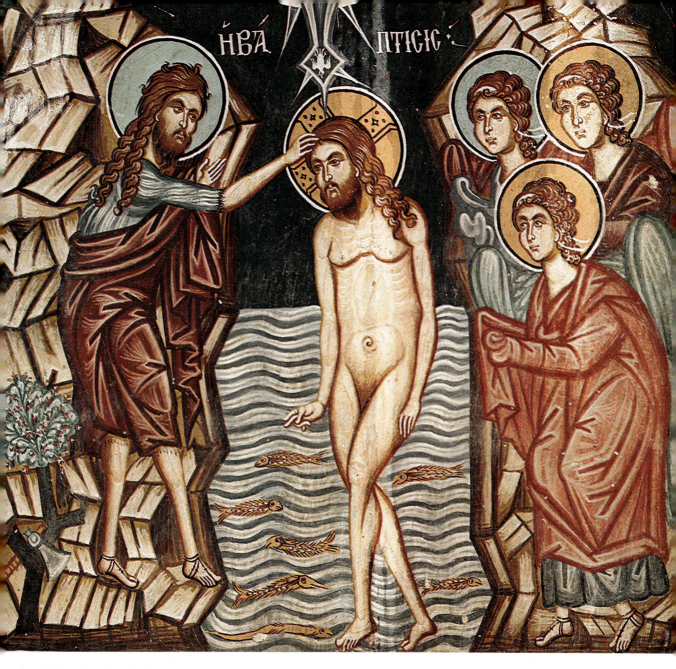

John baptized his cousin Jesus in the waters of the River Jordan.

Tradition tells us that John was a cousin of Jesus. John was also a preacher and many people followed him. John's message to the people was 'Reform your lives!' John baptized people in water as a sign that they would change their lives. Jesus, too, was baptized by John early in his ministry.

Peter and Andrew were among those chosen by Jesus to share his work of preaching and healing.

Following Jesus' baptism, he chose some men who were to be his special followers. There were twelve of them—mostly fishermen, and it was these men who gave up their livelihoods to work with Jesus and who would continue Jesus' ministry in the world. These men came to be called apostles. The names of the apostles were Peter, Andrew, James the Greater, John, Philip, Bartholomew, Thomas, Matthew, James the Lesser, Jude Thaddeus, Simon, and Judas Iscariot. Jesus chose Peter to head his church.

In faraway places, Jesus provided more than enough food for the crowd gathered around him in miraculous ways.

The Gospels, one of the first four books of the New Testament, are full of wonderful stories of Jesus and his apostles. And in each of the stories we can see how much Jesus loved the people.

One story tells how 5000 people had gathered to hear Jesus preach. They stayed and listened all day. By nightfall they were tired and hungry. Jesus did not want to send them away without food. But how could he feed so many people?

Tradition tells us that a boy there had 5 loaves of bread and 2 fish. Jesus took the food and blessed it. He told the apostles to give it out to the people. Even though they did not understand, they began to give out the food. And the baskets never became empty! All of the people were fed and when the fragments were gathered up, they filled 12 baskets! Jesus had worked a miracle.

There are even stories of Jesus bringing people back to life. One of these stories tells how Jesus was walking through the town of Naim when a funeral passed by. The person being buried was the only son of a widowed mother. Now she was all alone in the world. Jesus was filled with compassion for her and so he raised her son from the dead. Jesus' miracles astonished everyone and he became famous.

31

A hero's welcome: a criminal's execution

People want to make Jesus King and to fight the Romans under his leadership . . . Politicians and priests grow jealous of Jesus' influence . . . He enters Jerusalem in glory but is soon arrested . . He is condemned to death and crucified . . . He rises from death.

Gradually in Jesus' ministry two things began to happen. The first was that people began to hear about Jesus and came to follow him. They saw in Jesus a chance to gain power. They wanted to make him king and under his leadership fight the Romans and end their rule over the Jews. They wanted Jesus to save them from their oppression.

Jesus however, wanted no part in this. He did not want to be a political leader. He saw himself as a man of God whose kingdom was not on earth, but in heaven. His followers did not really understand this.

The second was that both the religious and political leaders of the day were becoming frightened of the power Jesus seemed to have over the people. They realized that his followers wanted to make Jesus king. The leaders knew that they must somehow get rid of Jesus. But they also knew that they must be very careful for Jesus' followers were numerous and they could easily be incited. Both the Romans and the Jews agreed that Jesus had to be stopped.

At about this time Jesus and his apostles went to Jerusalem to celebrate the feast of Passover. As they entered the city Jesus, who was riding on a donkey, was cheered by throngs of people who spread their cloaks on the ground and waved palm branches at him as though they were welcoming their king.

Jesus and the money-changers

A day or two after Jesus rode into Jerusalem he went to the temple to pray. The temple was considered a very holy and sacred place since it was the house of God. When Jesus arrived at the temple he found a great commotion there. People were not praying at all. Instead they were exchanging money, buying and selling animals to be sacrificed and using the temple area to carry on all sorts of business.

Jesus entered Jerusalem on a donkey, not a mighty war-horse. Here, at last, was the peaceful Messiah.

The money-changers and traders were driven from the Temple. 'You have turned my father's house into a den of thieves', Jesus scolded.

Jesus became angry. He saw the men turning the house of God into a marketplace. He drove the animal merchants out of the temple. He tipped over the tables of the money-changers and scattered their coins all about. He told them that they had made the temple a den of thieves.

This of course angered the leaders even more. They could no longer tolerate Jesus. The time had come to put an end to Jesus and his work. The leaders had had enough of his stories, his miracles, and his power.

Jesus is betrayed

The chief priests of the temple made arrangements to have Jesus arrested. Judas, one of the apostles, was given 30 pieces of silver in return for helping the soldiers to capture Jesus.

On Thursday, Jesus and the apostles gathered together to celebrate the Jewish feast of Passover. Jesus was aware that he would soon die. He knew that the authorities could no longer tolerate him. It was with a heavy heart that Jesus ate this last supper with his friends. He warned them that he was soon to die. He told them to always love each other and to continue to tell others of God's love. He shared bread and wine with them and told them to remember him whenever they shared this special meal. Then he prayed for them.

After dinner Jesus and his apostles went to a garden where they often went to pray. The Gospels tell us that Jesus was frightened as he prayed, and as the night wore on and he continued to pray, even his friends could not stay awake with him.

Before dawn Judas entered the garden, leading some Roman soldiers. Judas went up to Jesus and kissed him. This was the signal for the soldiers to come forward and arrest Jesus which they did.

Jesus was brought before the Sanhedrin, the council of high priests. They questioned Jesus and accused him of many crimes. They brought witnesses who spoke against him. Throughout this entire mock trial Jesus remained silent. Finally the witnesses gave the high priests the information that they had wanted to hear—they said that Jesus had claimed to be the Messiah. This was blasphemy according to the high priests. They said that they had no further need of witnesses. They decided to have Jesus killed.

The Sanhedrin, however, did not have the power to put a man to death. For this they had to have the consent of the Roman governor, a man called Pilate. So Jesus was brought to him.

Judas greeted Jesus with a kiss: this was a sign for the mob to lead Jesus away to the High Priest.

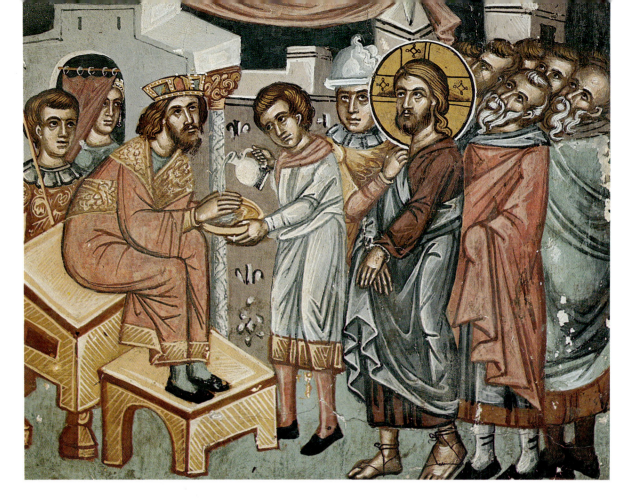

Pilate washed his hands in front of the crowd to show that he was not responsible for the death of Jesus.

Pilate was not at all concerned with Jesus' claim to be the Messiah, nor with the Sanhedrin's charge of blasphemy. What did concern him was whether Jesus was threatening Roman rule. He questioned Jesus but Jesus remained silent. Pilate thought Jesus was an innocent man and went to his balcony to tell the crowd gathered outside that Jesus should go free. The crowd however, had turned against Jesus and shouted 'Crucify him!' This was a common form of execution for criminals of the day. Finally, fearing a riot, Pilate handed Jesus over to be killed.

He was brought to a hill called Golgotha where he was nailed to a cross and died. Tradition tells us that Mary his mother and John his apostle were among those few who stayed with him until the end. He was

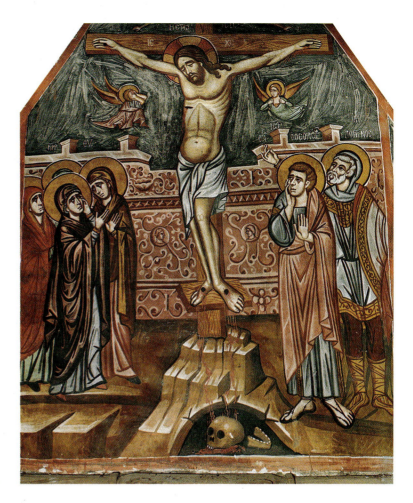

The peaceful Messiah was executed as a common criminal, labelled 'Jesus of Nazareth, King of the Jews'.

taken down from the cross and buried in a tomb donated by one of his followers.

What Christians believe happened three days later showed that Jesus' death on the cross was not at all the end of him, but only the beginning. Christians believe that on Sunday Jesus rose from the dead, that he came back to life. His followers saw him and ate with him. He appeared to them and to others. he stayed with them for a short time, perhaps forty days and then went to be with God in heaven. His followers began to believe what Christians today have as the center of their belief in Jesus—that he was the son of God.

Three days after Jesus had been taken from the cross, his body disappeared from its tomb. His followers claimed that he had come alive again.

They claimed he was God, and had come to earth in human form to die on the cross as a punishment for Man's wrongdoings. It was Man who deserved to be punished, not God, but God was loving and merciful and had therefore borne this punishment on Man's behalf.

Christianity has spread throughout the world and millions and millions of people throughout the ages have followed the teachings and kept alive the message of this man who so changed the world—Jesus.

The worship of Jesus Christ has spread throughout the world in many forms.

Dates and events

Scholars and historians have found it very difficult to give precise, and, in some cases, any, dates to the events in the life of Jesus Christ. The date of Jesus's birth has been based on the time which passed between the founding of Rome and the time of the census in Herod's reign. This puts the date of Jesus's birth at between 7 and 4 BC, though most historians give the year 4 BC.

The only other dates which can be given to events during and associated with the life of Jesus are:

6 BC	Judaea is annexed by Rome.
4 BC	Death of Herod. Judaea is divided among his sons.
6 AD	Judaea becomes a Roman province.
26 AD	Pontius Pilate is made Procurator of Judaea.
27 AD	Baptism of Jesus. He begins his ministry of preaching and healing.
28 AD	Execution of John the Baptist.
29 or 30 AD	Crucifixion of Jesus.

Mohammed

Mohammed unified the tribes of Arabia under the banner of a new religion. After his death his people conquered the greater part of the civilized world, spilling blood but rarely forcing acceptance of Islam—the faith which Mohammed had taught them. The religion Mohammed founded, fourteen centuries ago, is based on power and simplicity, the two great characteristics of its founder, Mohammed.

Mohammed was born in Mecca, in modern Saudi Arabia, about 570 years after Christ. In those days Mecca was always bustling with life and activity. Traders crowded into the city from every direction, some to pass through and some to sell their goods in its markets. In addition, thousands of people came every year to worship pagan gods in its holy places. The most famous of these was a building shaped like a giant dice and known as the Kaaba. In and around it were idols—probably one for every day of the year. At festival time the crags of the nearby mountains must have rung with the noise.

One day ten women came from the desert beyond the mountains. They were looking for babies to take away and nurse for their mothers. Nine of the women were successful in their search. As they rode off, the noise of their braying asses and squawking babies must have been terrible.

The woman they left behind was called Halima. The only baby she could find was little Mohammed, but Mohammed's widowed mother could not afford to pay her properly. At last Halima did take Mohammed and rode away with the child in her arms.

By the time Mohammed was four or five, he was able to help Halima's husband by guarding the sheep

This early illustration of the birth of the prophet reflects the tradition that the face of Mohammed is never depicted.

and gathering fodder. One day, expecting to find Mohammed carrying out his tasks, Halima found the child trembling with terror. He said some men in white had come and somehow touched him inside his chest.

'He must be falling ill,' said Halima's husband. 'He'll have to go back to his mother at once.' They hurried him home, with no idea that Mohammed's visions would change the world.

His mother decided Mohammed was perfectly well and asked him if he would like to go to Yathrib with her to stay with relatives. Mohammed was excited by the prospect: even the journey would be an adventure —a whole week riding a camel along the desert roads.

On the journey back to Mecca Mohammed's mother died. The heat of the sun often proved too great for travellers along the open desert roads. Mohammed was only six. For the next two years he was looked after by his grandfather and then, by his uncle, Abu Talib, whose home was also in Mecca.

Trading expeditions

As a baby, Mohammed had been afraid of the hubbub in the city streets. Now, as a growing boy, he began to understand it: people thought the way to please the gods was to shed the blood of animals in the holy places. The month of March was the really busy time in Mecca. The streets and open places were full of camels to ride, camels to kill and camels escaping from their owners. There were people chasing them, people dodging them, and people trying to buy and sell their wares without getting trampled by the animals.

It came as a relief when Mohammed left the city with Abu Talib on his trading expeditions. As they journeyed along the desert roads they sometimes saw

Traders crossing the desert would shelter at the caravanserai, a large inn with an enclosed courtyard.

a string of laden camels just like their own approaching from the distant hills. In the heat of the sun they would seem to tremble or disappear or float in the air. Mohammed and Abu Talib were glad the other travellers had got through the hills—it gave them hope that there were no robbers there. Sometimes, though, they came upon bodies, and then they passed

Mohammed and Abu Talib avoided robbers on their journeys and met people from other lands who believed in one God.

with fear the giant rocks that lay by the roadside. Robbers might be lurking, ready to pounce on their caravan.

So far as we know, Mohammed and Abu Talib were lucky. They were never attacked and, indeed, they met many interesting people on the road—people like the Jews and Christians of Syria, who believed in only one God. This must have seemed very strange to a boy from Mecca. In his teens Mohammed came to believe, as they did, in a single God, though it is unlikely that he let this belief be known.

Khadija's offer of marriage

Mohammed's trading expeditions were important in another way. The skill he had gained in buying and selling earned him a job—and a wife as well. He was in his twenties when a wealthy Meccan widow named Khadija asked him to travel with her goods into far-off lands. Soon, instead of riding together, he and his uncle were passing on the desert roads.

The archangels brought messages from God. They told Mohammed that he was the Messenger of Allah.

One day, Khadija sent one of her servants to ask Mohammed if he would marry her. She was a lot older than Mohammed, but she was very rich. Mohammed accepted. He could now live an easier life than ever before. Even so, he was restless: he wanted to find out more about God. Sometimes he disappeared to the mountains and sheltered for several nights in a cave, away from the noise and commotion of Mecca. There he thought and prayed in the hope that the truth would be revealed to him.

Messages from God

One day he heard a mysterious voice. 'You are the Messenger of Allah,' it said. (In Mohammed's language Allah meant God.) Mohammed tells how shocked he was: 'I was standing, but I fell on my knees and dragged myself along while the upper part of my chest was trembling. I got myself home to Khadija and said "Cover me! Cover me!" until the terror had left me.'

Sometimes strange things happened even when Mohammed was not in his cave. He might be talking to friends or riding his camel when suddenly he would hear a sound of chains or bells or rushing wings and fall to the ground, sweating, shuddering and becoming unconscious.

Some people thought Mohammed was ill, as they had done before. Mohammed himself was deeply troubled and upset by these happenings. 'I considered throwing myself from the top of a crag,' he later confessed.

Often, Mohammed saw an angel or archangel standing before him. It insisted that the visions and voices were real. Khadija was already sure of this and so was her cousin, a holy man whose opinions they trusted. Mohammed's adopted son and a merchant called Abu Bakr were also among the first to believe that Mohammed had special contact with God.

If Mohammed was Allah's Messenger, he must take good care to remember these messages God conveyed to him. It was his task to pass them on to everyone else. So, to keep them safe and unchanged, he and his friends began to write them on scraps of

These Indian girls are learning to read the Koran, the holy book which contains the messages that God sent to Mohammed.

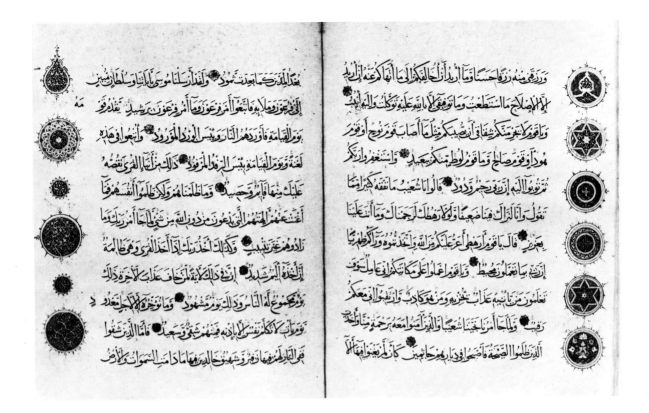

The messages now contained in the Koran were originally written down on scraps of leather, camel-bones and pieces of pottery.

leather, camel-bones, pieces of pottery, palm-leaves and so on. Later, they were gathered together in a holy book, which is called the Koran.

The announcement that Mohammed was the Messenger of God, though simple, was extremely important. It underlined the oneness of God and made the messages Allah's rather than merely Mohammed's. The oneness of God was a link with the Jewish and Christian religions which later messages emphasized. One went as follows: 'Say ye: "We believe in God . . . and in that which has been revealed to Moses and to Jesus . . . No difference do we make between any of them . . . " '

Because of their sympathy with the Jews, for some time Mohammed's followers faced Jerusalem for the prayers they said several times a day. This good feeling later changed into open hostility.

'City of the Prophet' welcomes Mohammed

The Meccans torment Mohammed's followers . . . He teaches about the life after death . . . Some followers come from Yathrib as pilgrims . . . Mohammed makes the secret pact of Aqaba with them . . . The Emigration —Mohammed escapes . . . Hardships afflict the Moslems in Yathrib . . . Conflict between the Meccans and Jews.

Mohammed's band of followers grew, though other Meccans tormented them cruelly. A man who claimed Mohammed was right and Allah was the only God was beaten till he changed his mind. Most Meccans feared that the spread of Mohammed's ideas would put an end to the worship of the pagan gods at the city's holy buildings and wells. Without the pilgrims, the traders' stalls and shops would not have many customers.

People made fun of Mohammed's teaching that one day the dead would come back to life. They would come back not as spirits, he said, but with their bodies, and Allah would send the good to heaven and the wicked to hell. People asked how bodies that had turned to dust could possibly return as flesh and blood. Mohammed answered that God had made us all in the first place, so he must be able to make us again.

The logic of his answers only angered those who did not share his beliefs. Even so, no one tried to kill him or to harm him. His uncle, Abu Talib, was an important man in Mecca, and no one would dare to injure his nephew, even now that he lived with Khadija. But when, in 619, Abu Talib died, Mohammed began to live in fear. Sometimes people threw things at him. Mohammed knew that worse things were likely to happen in the future.

Mohammed's vow

Early in 622, the pilgrimage season brought the usual hordes of idol-worshippers crowding into Mecca from all over Arabia. The pilgrims from Yathrib were those of Mohammed's followers who had been converted to Mohammed's beliefs during previous visits. They came to the holy places to worship Allah, not the many idol-gods that others respected. At the end of their visit, they slipped away from the other people of Yathrib—they had all

Mohammed is shown here with the first of his followers, Abu Bekir, Osman and Ali.

camped together outside the city—and assembled in the nearby valley of Aqaba, where Mohammed met them in the dead of night. He said that he and his Meccan followers who lived there already would vow to protect them. Their leaders promised this in their customary way of confirming agreements, each in turn striking Mohammed's hand once.

Thousands of pilgrims face the Kaaba, the black, dice-shaped building in Mecca which contained the many pagan idols.

Besides having converts in Yathrib, Mohammed knew there were many Jews and a number of Christians among its people. They would probably be converted quite easily.

Mohammed asked the Meccan followers to leave the city quietly, in little groups on separate days. They did as he asked, disappearing from Mecca in July, August and September. The year was 622, if we count from the birth of Christ, and Mohammed was about 52 years old. Moslems (people who follow Mohammed's teachings) know it as the year of the

Mohammed washes his hands before prayer, a tradition which Moslems have followed to the present day.

emigration, or Hegira, and count their years from then.

The daring escape

Mohammed stayed behind in Mecca to see his followers safely on their way. The Meccans must have known they were going and, in some ways, they were glad to be rid of them. Even so, they did not want Mohammed to leave as well. The best way to harm the Moslems, they had decided, was to deprive them of their leader.

Mohammed worked out a plan of escape. He and Abu Bakr, who had also stayed behind in Mecca, got themselves a guide and some camels. One day they slipped out of Mecca and headed southwards, away from Yathrib. For three days they hid in a mountain cave while the Meccans chased northwards towards Yathrib expecting to catch them. Then they headed

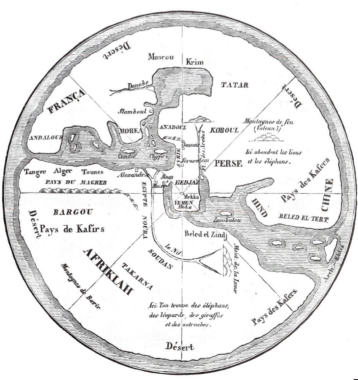

This twelfth-century Arabic map shows Mecca as the centre of the known world.

The tradition of building magnificent mosques such as this, the Blue Mosque in Istanbul, sprang from the building of Mohammed's courtyard in Yathrib.

towards Yathrib themselves by a secret route. After ten days' riding they arrived on the outskirts and sank down exhausted in the shade of a palm tree.

A few days later Mohammed bought a patch of land near the centre of the scattered settlement. This was to be the site for a courtyard. (It was also the start of the Moslems' tradition of building magnificent mosques.) Mohammed and his followers built the walls. Inside, up against one of the walls, they constructed a hut for Mohammed's wife. Khadija had died but Mohammed had subsequently married a widow called Sawda. Soon he would have an extra wife—Abu Bakr's daughter Ayisha. (By the time he died he had had some nine wives.) Mohammed never had more than four wives at any one time, and this has since become an accepted Moslem practice.

Ayisha was only a child when she married Mohammed, but she never forgot her wedding day. She was playing on a swing when someone came to get her ready for the ceremony. Her husband proved to be very kind—he let her keep her toys and dolls and sometimes even played games with her.

Mohammed defeats his enemies

In some ways, though, her life was hard. Mohammed and his followers were very poor. The other people who lived in Yathrib had date plantations. The Moslems' only land was their courtyard, where those who were homeless had to camp. Some earned a little money by watering date-palms. It was tiring work, especially drawing the water from wells.

At last, in 623, they were forced to start attacking and robbing Meccan merchants as they travelled on the desert roads. In the following year this led to a battle. A convoy of laden camels was on its way to Mecca. It would have to pass near to Yathrib and Mohammed's men lay in ambush near a group of wells the travellers would normally use. But the

Mohammed's men dug a ditch between Yathrib and the enemy forces, and used the soil to build a bank.

Some of the prophet's enemies went into battle mounted on elephants.

convoy was led by a clever man. He noticed some camel droppings with date stones in them. The camel must surely have come from Yathrib, and probably with a spy on its back. He told his convoy to hurry on —by a route that took them clear of the wells. At the same time someone galloped ahead to Mecca and raised an army. It rode to the wells, where Mohammed's men were expecting to find only a convoy of camels. Despite the shock they must have received, they acted wisely. They filled in all the wells but one and camped beside it. The Meccans needed water so they had to start fighting, even though the glare of the sun was in their eyes and the land was uneven. They lost the struggle in spite of their strength. The Moslems had won by clever tactics and skilful archery.

In 627 the Meccans came again with a massive army of 10,000 men. This time Mohammed prevented bloodshed by digging a ditch between Yathrib and the enemy forces. His men used the soil from the ditch to make a bank. They could either shelter behind it or stand on top. If the Meccans charged, they would have to go down into the ditch then scramble right to the top of the bank while Mohammed's men attacked from above. In the end the Meccans went away and never threatened Yathrib again.

Medina, 'City of the Prophet'

Successes like this led the people of Yathrib, including some who had not accepted Islam, to accept Mohammed's leadership. Even the chiefs of neighbouring tribes acknowledged him as overlord. As a sign of Mohammed's importance, Yathrib gained a new name; it came to be called Medina, a shortened form of the Arabic words for 'City of the Prophet'.

Mohammed taught that all men were brothers, and equal in the sight of God, but he also taught that fighting and war were justified under certain conditions. Force played a part in the growth of his power, but it seems rather strange that he used it against the Jews of Medina. He had thought of the Jews as allies and potential converts, as they worshipped the same God. In the event, they disagreed with the way he interpreted some of the scriptures. He taught that the Biblical figure Abraham was the forefather both of the Jews and of the Arabs. He also taught that he himself was Abraham's true successor as teacher and prophet. Ever since then Moslems have faced towards Mecca instead of Jerusalem when saying their prayers: a lasting sign of the rift that followed the Jews' disagreement.

The Mosque of the Prophet, Medina.

55

Mecca accepts the authority of Mohammed

Mohammed goes to Mecca as a pilgrim . . . The Meccans keep him out of the city . . . He returns and makes his pilgrimage . . . The next year he takes over the city . . . He rids the Kaaba of idols . . . He makes a final visit before his illness and death . . . The ultimate triumph.

It was now the year 628—the sixth year since the move to Medina. Mohammed had not gone back to Mecca in all this time. He had even missed the yearly festival. Had he wanted to attend this pagan celebration, the Meccans would have kept him out. Had he tried to enter the city, they would probably have killed him. This annoyed Mohammed. Mecca was his birthplace and he had lived there over half his life. Why should he have to stay away? It was risky to go to the city, but his growing importance might save him from harm. And his fame would increase if people saw that others were afraid to hurt him. What was more, he would have the chance to preach about Allah. One day, he hoped, everyone would worship Allah, and the pagan gods would be forgotten.

The return to Mecca

Mohammed invited his followers to go to Mecca with him. Altogether a thousand Medinans rode off into the desert on their horses and camels. After nearly a week, they arrived by night in the hills a few kilometres north of Mecca. They lit themselves bonfires, and scouts rode out of the city to see who was coming. When they realized that Mohammed was there with a thousand men, they armed themselves and prepared for battle. Then, as the sun came up, they saw that none of Mohammed's men was in wargear. They had not even brought their bows and arrows. Instead, they had with them some animals for sacrifice, and a few of their womenfolk. The Meccans were confused—their enemy had come in peace. But should they allow the Moslems to join in a pagan festival? The famous *hajj*, or pilgrimage, was due to begin.

At last, despite much loud argument, the Moslems and Meccans made a peaceful decision. Mohammed and his followers would stay away this year, but next year they would have the city to themselves for three

*When Mohammed returned to Mecca after seven
years, he rode his white camel solemnly around the
Kaaba.*

days and nights.

When the time came, they rode into Mecca like conquerors. The city was almost deserted, but the Meccans watched from the neighbouring hills as Mohammed—back after seven years—rode his white camel solemnly around the Kaaba. He passed seven times between the mounds that stood nearby. His people followed on foot and cried 'Behold, I am yours! Behold, I am yours!' After these rituals, one of Mohammed's followers climbed up onto the roof of the Kaaba and called the people to prayer. (Nowadays, Moslems are called to prayer from the tower, or minaret, of their mosque.)

The Meccans were so impressed and frightened by Mohammed's power and authority that the following year they allowed him to take the city over, this time for good. The Meccans would live there, but Mohammed would rule them.

Moslem converts

Once again he entered in triumph. The Meccans watched from their roofs and balconies as Mohammed touched the black stone of the Kaaba. This was a stone from heaven—a meteorite. It was probably the most sacred of all the sacred things in Mecca. As he touched it, he cried out 'Allahu akbar'—Allah is greatest. He entered the Kaaba and ordered that the idols should be destroyed and the pagan pictures taken away. Finally, before riding home, he called on the Meccans to accept him as Allah's Messenger and sat on a rock as they filed past and paid homage. At least they knew the fears they had had in the first place were unfounded—Mohammed would not prevent people from coming to Mecca as pilgrims. He was turning the pagan pilgrims into Moslem pilgrims.

In 632 Mohammed made a final visit to Mecca. He was making sure that the rituals were all being

The muezzin, the official of the mosque, calls the people to prayer in Istanbul.

performed in the name of Allah. Soon after getting home from Mecca, he fell ill. At first he tried to carry on as though nothing was wrong. By day he worked and prayed as usual, though pain sometimes made him cry out aloud. His legs were unsteady and he had a bandage round his head.

At last he was forced to stay in bed. He chose Ayisha's hut, and his favourite wife became his

Inside the Blue Mosque, Turks pray by the mimbar, the preacher's pulpit.

nurse. Once, when his followers were in the court- yard praying, he dragged himself up and threw back the curtain that covered Ayisha's doorway. His

followers saw him standing there and smiling at them. They thought he was recovering, but they were never to see their leader again.

News of his death caused grief and confusion among the Medinans. Some could not believe it had happened. Others believed it and felt afraid. Without a strong leader, the Medinans and Meccans were likely to quarrel. And, if this happened, Mohammed's work would end in confusion. Who should they choose in Mohammed's place? The Medinan people argued about it into the night. At last they chose Abu Bakr, the man who had helped Mohammed to make his daring escape from Mecca.

Bakr was the powerful leader they needed. With the help of skilful commanders, he quelled a rising of Arab tribes which followed the news of Mohammed's death. He then began the great Arab expansion which carried Islam far outside its original homeland.

Mohammed's death brought both grief and confusion to the Medinans. They had lost their leader.

Dates and events

The life of Mohammed is perhaps the best documented of the three great prophets. Accounts were written shortly after Mohammed's death, and the sources now used were based largely on those early writings.

570 AD Mohammed is born the son of a poor merchant. His father died soon after Mohammed's birth.

576 AD Death of Mohammed's mother. Mohammed goes to live with his uncle Abu Talib.

594 AD Mohammed enters the service of Khadija, a rich widow, whom he marries.

610 AD Gabriel appears to Mohammed at the mountain Hira, near Mecca. He commands Mohammed to preach the true religion.

614 AD He receives the command from God to preach to the people.

622 AD Mohammed flees to Medina. He becomes ruler of the city and sanctions war against the enemies of Islam, especially the Meccans.

623 AD First battle between the Moslems and Meccans is fought at Badr. The Moslems are victorious.

625 AD Meccans defeat Moslems at Ohod.

627 AD The siege of Medina.

628 AD Mohammed makes peace with the Meccans and is recognized as chief and prophet.

632 AD Mohammed's last pilgrimage to Mecca. Later that year he dies.

Glossary

Baptism A Christian ceremony. A person is immersed in or sprinkled with water as a sign of being cleansed of sin and becoming a member of the Church.

Convert A person who has changed his or her belief to another religion.

Disciple One of the personal followers of a religious leader.

Healer A person who restores others to good health, not always by medical means.

Hegira The flight of Mohammed from Mecca to Medina in AD 622. This became the starting point of the Moslem era.

Hermit Any person who lives their life alone.

Idol-worship Admiring or revering a carved figure or object as if it were a god.

Islam The religion of Moslems based on the teachings of Mohammed.

Koran The sacred scripture believed by Moslems to be the word of God dictated to Mohammed by an angel.

Meditate To control all thoughts or to think deeply about something.

Messiah The awaited King of the Jews, to be sent by God to free them. Christians believe Jesus Christ to be this figure.

Monastery A place where monks or nuns can live a religious life away from the rest of society.

Monsoon Seasonal wind of South Asia bringing with it heavy rain.

Pagan Anything connected with a religion other than Christianity, Islam or Judaism.

Pagoda A temple found in India or the Far East, usually a tower in the shape of a pyramid.

Pilgrimage Journey to a shrine or sacred place as an act of religious devotion.

Prophet A holy man through whom God reveals his will.

Saint A very holy or good person held in high esteem for their deeds or behaviour.

Scriptures Writings which are very sacred or holy.

Vision A mystical or religious experience that can come to a person.

Further reading

The Buddha and Buddhism
The Buddha, Michael Pye
  (Biblio Distributors, 1979)
Buddhism, (A First Book), I. G. Edmonds
  (Franklin Watts, 1978)
The Prince Who Gave Up a Throne:
  A Story of the Buddha,
  Nancy Serage
  (Harper and Row, 1966)

Christ and Christianity
Today's Story of Jesus, David L. Edwards
  (Collins, 1976)
The Man of Galilee, Clifford Stevens
  (Our Sunday Visitor, 1979)
A History of Christianity, Paul Johnson
  (Atheneum Publishers, 1979)
Twenty Centuries of Christianity, Maureen
  Curley, (Pflaum Press, 1977)

Mohammed and Islam
The World of Islam, Richard Tames
  (Viking Press, 1967)
Islam, I. G. Edmonds
  (Franklin Watts, 1977)
The Story of Mohammed the Prophet,
  Bilzik Alladin, (Auromere, 1979)

Index

Picture acknowledgements

The publishers would like to acknowledge all those who provided the pictures which illustrate this book on the following pages: Alan Hutchison Library 15, 21; British Museum 47; Hilary Gibson 6, 7, 9, 10, 13, 14, 18, 19 (below), 20 (above); Mansell Collection 12, 16; Mary Evans Picture Library 50; Michael Holford Library 4, 11, 19 (above); Sonia Halliday Photographs front cover, 20 (below) photographed by Jane Taylor, 22, 24 (above), 25, 26 photographed by Sonia Halliday and Laura Lushington, 29, 30 stained glass window by Gabriel Loire—photographed by Sonia Halliday and Laura Lushington, 31, 33, 35, 36, 37, 38, 39, 40, 42, 43, 1840 engraving by Thomas Allom—hand painted by Laura Lushington, 44 photographed by James Wellard, 45, 49, 51 (above), 52, 54 (left and right), 57, 59, 60, 61.